G000299070

Praise for
**Wendy Taylor Carlis**
*Reading Berryman to t*

"The poems of Wendy Taylor Carlisle are vibrant, original, intelligent, tough, funny, and sharp as a first-time blade. I admire them utterly. They do not contain a single extra word. They have the power to transport, to remind, in all the best senses of that word, re-mind to uplift and enlarge the mental faculties to a finer degree of sensibility.... I appreciate the heat and summer here. That's one lucky dog."

—Naomi Shihab Nye, former chancellor of
the Academy of American Poets

" 'The body stores it all,' writes Wendy Taylor Carlisle. In this strong collection, the mother brakes at a stop sign and flings her arm across the child's chest, the dead 'never lay their fingers on a sunburned arm,' and the lover 'invade[s] her nostrils as a hot, metallic smell.' From classical reference to personal recollection, the poems in *Reading Berryman to the Dog* are vivid and immediate."

—Penelope Scambly Schott, author of
*Waving Fly Swatters at Angels*

**Praise for
Wendy Taylor Carlisle:**

"The history, deep south surroundings, and personal convictions of poet Wendy Taylor Carlisle are a collective wonder to behold."

—Gabriel Ricard, *Drunk Monkeys* review of
*The Mercy of Traffic*

# Reading Berryman to the Dog

# Reading Berryman to the Dog

# Poems
# Wendy Taylor Carlisle

BELLE
POINT
PRESS

Fort Smith, Arkansas

READING BERRYMAN TO THE DOG

Edited by Casie Dodd
Design & typography by Belle Point Press

Belle Point Press
Fort Smith, Arkansas
bellepointpress.com
editor@bellepointpress.com

Cover image (dog): Mithul Varshan, via Pexels

An earlier version of this collection was published in 2000
by Jacaranda Press, San Jose, California

Printed in the United States of America

ISBN: 979-8-9858965-6-5

RBD/BPP6
1.1

*With gratitude to Andrea, Phil, and Naomi, my readers: Tamam,*
*Selena, Linda, Willie; my family: David, Sam & Sam, and Rick;*
*and to Margo & Jean, who put it together,*
*and Casie Dodd, who revived it.*

## Compline

Each night I say it, the prayer for silence,
for no whiskey sighs, no pewter rain
in the mountains, no granite storm's
bedlam on the folded tin roof, no squandered
children under a heavy downpour.

This is a small prayer, Lord.
Keep us from the breathing scream, the stones
falling and falling.

# Contents

## Home Fires

At the gates Peleus' boy, the one with the bad heel,
waits for his war. The Gods know his mother

tried to save him to make her mixed marriage last.
Six children sacrificed, the ardent goddess

blazed to purge her seventh of mortality,
but where she held him didn't scald.

Out of childhood's shadow, he doesn't feel
his own weak foot; he can't recall the flame,

the stranger's bone. Eager for vengeance,
not enticed to live forever out of the fire, he hefts

the great round shield, his principal defense
his mother's love. Underneath his breastplate

what is mortal and almost mortal thrums.
He doesn't notice how the touched place burns.

# Notes for a Childhood I

i.

Words with no meanings—
hibiscus, yes, bougainvillea, croton
and the others, trade winds, Sergeant Majors.
At the edge of the known the octopus
turned inside-out to pink, the nuns
who comb our tangled hair each afternoon
on the porch. Octo is eight,
says mamma and the nuns are named
Sister Owen Phillip, Sister Immaculata.
Even the saccharine smell under the rubber
cone has a name: ether. I need
a word for my hand, for a certain
sort of skin that, surface warm, contains
such cold I shiver every time I look.

ii.

Without looking she slung her forearm
across my middle in those days before
seatbelts when she careened up to
each stop sign as if it would melt
under her cold eye. No.
They always stayed put and warranted
that arm athwart the front seat,
the reliable OOF of a small unwilling chest,
its air puffed out, and God help us
if I hit the dash—the metal hard as sin—
and wore the bruise because of her slow arm

too late to save me. From mamma, I learn
to race toward whatever stops us hating it,
slamming the brakes at the last instant.

iii.

An instant of twirling, hair slung in slow motion,
skirt a vivid absence of color spun out
in abundant circles like the hub of a childhood,
chestnut and sharkskin in that perfect moment
of turning. No screaming. No sweet, sick smell.
No veins on her neck pulsing. Instead,
mamma spins, arms held out like the wings on a B52,
slim fingers curled in, palming the secret
of what a hand might do. Beautiful. Silent.
Turning in the land of '47 Chevys, Eisenhower
and the GI Bill. Like America after the war,
running right up to the edge,
her breath jarred loose by Buck Rogers,
her future flung forward into decades of fists.

## Free Fall

She tumbles through the atmosphere arms out,
dancing with migratory loons—
cuts through the clouds, gaining detail

secured by silk no more substantial
than a dream of being rocked. She dives
wild until the rip, jolt, sway—

the mild sun stroking the translucent
umbrella, her shadow beneath, lines thin as
shoestrings, mooring her to the day

while rigid pines jump up to meet her.
It was always like this—
held by cords she could barely see, vivid motion

the snap of stop. At last, the silk billowing
over her, her ears filled with rustle and hiss,
the harness impossible to slip.

## Penelope

Getting older with each day's shuttle.
There's never a moment's peace, just shove and hustle.
The only supple thing here is my hands—it's lanolin, I guess.

Sweet Minerva, I need a novel prank, new jest, anything
to keep the suitors' hands off, keep 'em pacified.
When Amphinomus brushed an eager palm

against my thigh, I all but jumped out of my dress.
I sit straight, clasp the family honor close, whereas they
love me loud and raucous, chiefly for my real estate.

How could I hit the mattress with one of these
brazen hunks, although their chests are smooth and taut,
with my Odysseus so good in bed? I think I recall that.

Some say I have a magic loom, undoing each day's doing—
but no one's there at night as I unravel, tear deep in.

# *Start a Journal*

Begin with evening on the bayou,
Black Jack in a Ball jar, borrowed Marlboros.
Describe the sound of the Atchafalaya,
The yelp of hounds back in the swamp.
Add bits of conversation, opinions on liars
And politicians. Complain about reporters
And the state of the art. Tell it all.
Be brazen. How Mother calls too often
And you hate it. Share that part.
Put a date on it: summer.
Spill gin and tonic on the cover.
Do this quick, before the light goes,
Before the day narrows down
To the creek bed, the water running away.

## *What Was It to Snow White?*

The shape of the mirror
  a walk in the woods
    the homecoming

rendered in miniature
  seven little stories
    like the nip of conscience.

The trade-off
  for three hots and a cot?
    Polish fourteen boots

pull seven custodial twelves
  tangled in dishrags
    end up exhausted

ravenous. For a Rome Beauty
  then, it was nothing
    to open the door.

Glass-encased after, what mattered?
  Her reflection.
    The cost of the fruit.

## Kissing the Frog

At the all-night Pancake House,
the plastic seats cracked
and the water glasses etched

by 1000 washings, we connect
eagerly, hurried in from
opposite directions, pale and damp.

At home, we each have
someone perfect we can't trust—
striped shirts, blond wrists.

Hunched over our cups,
we recall mouth-watering days
at the river. Mayflies hovered

on slack eddies, the sun
leached all colors to olive drab.
Should I ask if you still believe

in wet kisses rising
to the surface like catfish?
Should I say

I'm still the same hungry princess
prying at the sticky menu
where I wish to find our story,

read it out loud and discover
what comes after happy.
Is it the picture of me lying

on your chest?
The slithery touch? Is it the kiss
that changes your face?

Imagine us. How it would be
to open our ribs,
to gather in the small, dark frogs.

## Wolf

It is not hunger or its empty howl
He fears. It's the helpless taste for pork

That propels and masters him.
Hog lust eating up the night, chewing

Through the dark to their tidy houses.
Straw, then sticks, then brick, he

Admires the walls, imagines them
Blown away, razed, pictures pig families,

Sees them light lamps, tell tales, bear young.
He craves them skewered,

Bar-b-qued to ease his fearful appetite.
At night he tells himself that sows

Are born fools. That pigs exist to tempt
A wolf. He knows he is a fiend

To get at them, will chance a steep climb
To the chimney to catch the smell

Of their rank, sweet hides: useless swine,
Pigs, prey, will slide to their center—

Their hot, sweet center.

# I Swan

*A sudden blow: the great wings beating still . . .*
—William Butler Yeats

Everyone makes much of it but truth to tell
the honor could have had more physical appeal.
Trumpeters have limited romantic skills
and lack imagination, not to mention lips.

During the act, I must admit I entertained
some questions of a theologic nature.
The poets say he overwhelmed me on that bank—

the sudden blow, the storm of wings.
Why do they reckon I gave in? Inquisitive?
You bet. And let me say that even mediocre sex
can't take the edge off having done it with a God.

As for the kids, around the neighborhood
my alibi is this: they came from eggs.
Don't blame me if they didn't turn out good.

# The Mathematics of Hunger

All she knows adds up to
the insight of hand and lip, tallying
gnaw and gulp to swallow.

She tabulates by taste, pasta, bacon,
grits, then licks her fingers, digital
cartographers calibrating to a clean plate.

She reckons the seasons by the chafe of
frozen ears, a sunburned thigh, divides
by wind-whipped hair for the year's sum.

To cipher a man, she rolls flesh
in her mouth like a dumpling.

In the geometry of palm and tongue,
hunger is the first calculation.

# The City

*make the objects sitting before you into a little city.*
                                    —Lynn Emanuel

This is how you start. Turn left off the hall freeway. You'll
see first the small houses like stacked magazines, their dim
matchbox porches. Then the city. Or perhaps it may be only a
table-sized town, the largest buildings—Federal, Religious,
Medical—no more than cereal boxes. A milk carton clinic
appears, then neighborhoods, an undistinguished aggregate—
jam jars, a humidor, ruby red glasses. There is even a select-
man, his hands crammed in his khaki pockets. See him pulled
forward in a sociable lope through the snarled streets, their
slick cars tumbled like silverware in the intersections.

Is this a sad seeing? Is it too shabby and tangled? Ask yourself
how the days flashed and vanished like light reflected off a lac-
quer breakfast tray, like moving traffic. Then look at the table.
There you will find everything. All you need to finish this city.
This living.

# Notes for a Childhood II

i.

The body remembers everything:
music years out of date—
bop, rockabilly—
moving to it, the sheared hair
on a neck like a valentine,
the bitten edges of long-ago
nails, the scrape of plastic
bracelets on a wrist, the taste of
iron, smell of childhood skin.
The body feels again the sweat
under new breasts. The body
remembers wet, the lungs
growing larger and larger,
balloons of icy air, surrounding a cry.

ii.

If it weren't for his thick hair,
his thrilling match book collection,
he'd be just another fattish guy
in a bad suit, but his slicked-back
tide of graying waves kept calling
her eyes to his small patch of
naked scalp, his belly pushed
out beyond the buttons
on his polyester shirt.

Who'd believe he could do it,
a man who listened to baseball
on the radio, fought in Europe,
was glad to be home,
to put Brylcreem on his hair?

iii.

It was the never-do, like being
hungry after dinner or wide-awake
after the Lone Ranger.

It was the plainness of cotton sheets
for the body that believes what it is told,
behaves in a thin bed, taking care of itself,

not aching, not burning into the leaking
dark, not passing rows of Gorgon women
under Lovely Lady Salon metal hats,
who chatted about the things
they said could never, didn't, wouldn't
happen in families like theirs.

# Touch

*…vectors, which fix the way a thing / goes reeling according to
where it was touched.*

—Galway Kinnell

In contrary twilight, a child escaping
    sleep might slip through a board
        in the neighbor's fence,

or what postpones the night could be
    as simple as lying
        still in that gap between

the palm and the soft place it's seeking.
    When an ordinary hand comes
        this close, a space widens

between act and recall.
    The body stores it all. In recollection,
        curled hands their nails dug in-

to the pad of flesh below the thumb,
    a rigid spine. A child knows how to lie
        quiet, count her breath, let her chest

rise/fall/rise, steady as slumber,
    mute, praying no one dares
        to wake a sleeper and when

the floor whispers, can ease into inertia.
    Even after years, she still counts steps.
        Until a lifetime later,

in a room where curtains exhale
        over an open window and the sun
                escapes through the horizon,

in a neighborhood where noise
        burns away, on a day,
                which is also the present,

a woman can lie down
        loose in her body.
                A mild hand can reach out.

# Wildcatting

The redhead is a fool for love. This September
it's a driller from Houston. She trails him
east across a landscape etched with dickey birds.

Their metal beaks reach down, bounce back
like the glass canary she set rocking
in her grade-school kitchen. The bird illustrated

perpetual motion, moved by evaporation,
its head feather drifting idly. The redhead stares
from the pickup's cab while the steel birds

pulse over the wells, rolls in from Texas
in a reverie of lust, spinning to the Gulf
through Beaumont, Baton Rouge, Biloxi.

Ahead of her, over the hood, a crimson feather
pulls, dips, almost touches the water.

## The Redhead Married a Good Man

The redhead married a good man
twice. The second time she did it
the first man had been gone a year.

She knew some facts by then—
she knew that love leaves, love comes back,
that often it comes back while you are out

grocery shopping, at the laundromat.
She reckoned "good fight" was an oxymoron,
figured out how not to seem bored

and hoped that acting like
she loved a man, even if just then
it wasn't true, would do. As for the rest,

she hoped it was enough and
what came next was simple grace or luck.

## Naked

The fall your father died all the leaves came down
in a three-day rainstorm. It was a damned fine storm.
The rain went on steady, one day into the next, while
leaves fell slow and constant, regular as raindrops.
The last hay baled weeks before, farmers at the co-op
had nothing to do but nod and rock and spit, and watch
the trees strip, till they were naked in the carpeted fields.

You were thirty-four the year those wet hills unrolled, glossy
as a calendar picture, and you took your father's cancer
like you did the weather. Under the dripping eaves, your chair
tipped back, you talked about the hay, but you seemed slighter,
more like a boy, as if your father's passing gave you back
childhood, stripped you, washed you down. As if he
fathered you, dying, and you could be naked then, being his son.

## Notes on the Hereafter

No matter if birds invented clouds
or vice-versa.
It's a sure jolt to discover

the unlovely young—
cousins-in-law, road musicians,
some nephews—

will outlive us. All our howling
about fair, unheard.
Our private conundrums?

Still obscure.
Who cares? They're here.
We're gone.

At closing time, it hurts
to find that no one's
keeping score of

our good will or flaws, both
weightless then
as feathers on the Lethe.

# Questions

i.

How is it done?
One day in our rooms we occupy space,
the next we turn the corner.

In March you were there:
round, solid, wearing
a broad expanse of belly. By June

you were gone. Not waiting
at the filling station.

Not at Ballatos, idling
over coffee and flan.

Gone. The studio empty,
your shirts hanging flat
in a locked cedar closet.

ii.

How is it?
One day, in our flesh shirts—
constant, reliable—the next vanished

so suddenly, friends are dazed,
left to wait, lingering
over coffee and dessert.

iii.

How does it go after?
As it did after the death of friends,
pancakes for breakfast,

cardinals at the feeder,
nothing different beyond a slight
thickening of the air around your bed.

This summer, pitchers of lemonade
condense on a white slatted table
but I still can't abide the heat,

can't be sure I'm there
when I turn away from the mirror.
I must guess. Yes.

It all goes on without us.
Breakfast. Someone's reflection.
The heaviness of air.

## Dog Days

Along this county FM road there's water vapor
gathered in the ditches and overhead
the oaks show dusty green. The radio reports
on politics and fornication, a teacher
and her thirteen-year-old lover. Good folks
are stunned by gossip and hot weather.

Lord, save us from the need to chide sad flesh
or to believe we're not all animals with wishes.
Help us admit the blessing in an August wind,
a cloud-troweled sky, the shelf of blue behind.

Show us the truth's an urgent belly,
what we need most, the slick fender on a Chevy,
a body bent over it, hot as a summer garage,
the roller coaster second before we come.

## In a Grand Hotel

A woman in red lace, in slingbacks
lets one delicate crimson strap
slide down her humerus to the elbow,
opens her body—that book of joy—
and forgets for a moment all other hotels.

In this fable, a man fits his palm
to the ball of the woman's shoulder.

She does not remember, when she wakes
at three, that the phrase in her head
is a message that will not give up
its meaning. She will not unravel
what happened that night at the bar.

The woman is the sum of all these parts.

For her, the morning
when it comes rocks forward
into waking like a shoulder slipping free,
holds again the threat of embrace
and still fits into the day like
a ball into a socket, a hand to skin,
while in the hotel the air conditioner
hums its inscrutable hum.

## The Redhead Conjures Him Up

middle-aged by now—
standing on the porch of
the Berry Street house
where he first held her—
his cap toes pushed right up
to the oak front door,
his hand on the knocker's brass arm.

To help him strike it
she will make him a sign,
wear white, drive in the dark
with no headlights, whistle
a few bars of *Sincerely*.

Then he can spin
through the door, driving blind.
He can make his own sign,
croon *Funny Valentine*, declare
they are lovers still,
lovers and full of light.

# *Reasons for Yes*

because sailboats were remote canvas specks
because gulls flew from the rooftops

because in the sun a body smells languid
because the wind gigued

because oars lay in rusted oarlocks
because of empty sidewalks

because of favorable signs:
CHICK'S BISTRO 10 MINUTE MASSAGE,
     *Licensed Therapist on Duty*

because our bodies are 60% saltwater
and we are saved by the sea coming in

when we want to go out and vice versa
because we loitered in an ambient tide

## Keeping Up with the Dead

All around they multiply, push off from barrooms,
lie down on railroad tracks, wreck automobiles.

They tango out, fondling silk casket liners,
faces settled into rictus grins. I pretend not to notice.

I say the dead don't overrun my street. I heal
from the outside in, a puncture wound of loss

until I can't avoid the crowd, laminated on the inside
of my sunglasses, stacked like cordwood in my mind's backlot.

Although, post mortem loved ones have some serious flaws—
forget to buy ice cream on the way home, don't make it

to the kid's homeroom, never lay their fingers on a sunburned arm
or urge the sweaty hair back from a forehead with cool hands—

I love them anyway, knowing their promises were useless
as Houdini's, who once he passed could never make a sign.

## Seasonal Losses

Last summer's weathered hay, the splash of tires
on blacktop—fall rain shingles off an umbrella,
weeps from the cupola, makes a cool counterpoint
to the zealous blooming in his head—a cancer
that sets the milk carton on the lit stove,
shuffles into the garden naked as a rosebush.

Our dead in fall. Their absolute numbers,
heavier than I thought, than leaves piled
against the fence, their particular faces
reduced to one skeletal face, where gravity
pares away all that was supple, extra
until their passing requires only someone
to sit and watch the scant twist of flesh
from which inclination departs.

I drive into the fast-growing tumor of the city,
winter rye sprouting in sidewalk cracks,
the quick retractions of chill, shucked knees
and elbows—behind me under remaindered dirt,
beyond recognition, all that's left of fall,
the damaged stone, the austere moons of their nails.

## Missing Them

Did you think the Dead would end face up,
still as mud once you laid their stiff cuffs out?
Not likely.

There's a rhythm to what happens
on the ivory cushions: a bump, a slight shift,
a loosening of the funeral hair.

After they settle piecemeal, they rustle
in the gutter like newsprint, resonate
with the airy hiss of escape, not quite

asleep, diminished to background croon,
a murmur of long-ago radio thrillers. I hear them
across the brick back walls of childhood.

The Shadow. Mr. Moto. I tune in
to a remembered whisper, cruel words I still miss.

# Stories

He has the best stories, the Lieutenant—
tales of ears, dried-deaf and in a jar,
of wordless whores, the blood mist on his skin
in patterns like a cracked tattoo.

The green and pungent whir of jungles
he might tell about back home
in Arkansas. The soldier has all the lines.

His woman recollects him fresh
from bucking hay. He held her tight.

Recalls she prayed him out of sight
and wondered how she'd wait.
And if she didn't? Who remembers now
for eighteen months at eighteen,
if her time went fast or slow?

She can't complain, nothing leveled
or pillaged in Bee Branch. No landmines.

Just then—and for a long time after—
his best joke's on her.
She always says he breaks her up.

# The War

She had the war inside
so when he came with his napalm
his foreign women
it seemed only natural the fight would continue
their marriage the tunnel they twisted in
their breath hissing
like missiles over the perimeter
they fit together like hinge and pin
blew apart as easily as a mined knee
left the usual phantom limb

# Reading Berryman to the Dog

People say that dogs have souls but truthfully,
they're bloodthirsty as generals. My new dog—
one hundred pounds plus—treasures dried pig ears,

hoards them like a recruit. I hear him in the garage
shattering them, chewing. The dog flew in
on American Air with my sweaty tee shirt

in his crate for the smell. Still, we were strangers
when the front-end loader set him down,
and when I had to touch him, the day went slick

in my hand. I grubbed for a Ken'L bone,
crooned a safe-dog song. Years after Tet,
I loved a tall Marine who seldom spoke

about the war. In Asia, he had enemies
and friends he couldn't tell apart. In our bed,
he dreamed of napalm and demolished sleep.

The dog noses the furniture, uneasy
as a stranger at morning Mass; he measures
the cats' intent with a long stare. The Rottweiler

manual declares the breed is
*fond of small animals . . . . will, however, kill rabbits.*
After a decade, the soldier phoned.

His words made a fist sound in my ear.
The receiver slid in my palm. I listened to
his familiar voice, didn't hang up.

Now he phones sometimes. Sometimes I answer.
If I cry the dog stands close, waits
for the all-clear, then I take him out

to the porch, let his sad head rest on my foot
and read to him from Berryman, the *Opus Dei*,
the prayers, until he can finally sleep.

# The Burners: 1868/1996

the hard gallop across Porter's place,
north along Little Ben creek, dingy cabins
the mist, punk pine, the whoosh of tindery tarpaper
the burn smell in the woods for weeks

      when it's done, the sawgrass
      the logging path, the gas on your hand
      the way the pews smolder
      long after it's over

the stutter of white in the dense brush
the way the horses' breath steams out
the slow lope home, how you strut
how you bless your kinfolk

      the way the Ford could use a balance
      and wobbles at sixty so you don't speed
      the way you go in and hug the kids
      their faces shine with TV light

your family after, the way they
need you on the calm front porch
the way you love them,
the way you love them all

## Reunion

My hands gray in the shadow of the visit, frayed
cuticles, cold coffee and ink scratched into a knuckle.

Stretching from meal to meal the days passed—
dishes for four, her mouth greedy as a birdling.

Then, beyond the farewell flap, stillness,
an emptied room, my fingers at rest.

With only the chickens to cluck in congress
under the window, I am comfortless

until at last, her voice comes back—
querulous, apologetic—and I know

that her teeth, yellow and perfect,
are chewing and chewing again.

# Silence

At their first meeting she was shy until he sank down into her mouth and planted a smack on her that seeped through her hair and clothes, her pores, like fumes from an ether-soaked rag. She was hooked. Just that quick, he became her new best friend, her pungent, fiendish sweetheart. She cherished his tricks, how he slid a loving hand into her side, slithered along her viscera then crawled up her vagina already mute. She treasured their time together, how he'd invade her nostrils as a hot, metallic smell and climax in her brain through the ear canal, how she'd reach further and further into his stillness.

Her former lover asked questions and her father too, but she never said another word. He had moved in by then, set up house, and she focused first on inhaling and later, on how to let her breath go.

## Rocket Science

When Chickie and I climbed into the tree
to sit and wait for our periods,
Chickie was an optimist. I wasn't sure
mine would ever come. But it did
months after Chickie showed off
her belt, the hooks on each end. Swinging
her legs over the branch, she explained
how grown up felt more clearly than
our teacher did in her lecture,
"On Being a Woman," better
than the grainy black and white film
with its scientific diagrams—
the retort-shaped organ floating
in our girl bodies, the miniature
rockets our brothers were
always trying to get us to touch.

Chickie and I educated ourselves,
studied the pamphlets, got answers
from the books we read.
We believed in science then, in Apollo
and a manned moon. We believed
we had learned all we needed
to know about how it would go
with the boys. We imagined it
was an experiment in simple biology.

# San Miguel Widow

When he chose the formality of
bougainvillea and cathedral, mornings chill
and noon as thick as paste,
why did she follow him like a tourist?

*This is a city for widowhood*, she sighed,
*and I decline the weeds.*
As if she could outlaw his whims
and what came after with a ban.

Who could resist him then? Who would
believe his face ten years ago,
the clean planes of his cheek, his hair
short silk, a white that sucked up light?

She has new names to call his city now—
its hewn stone steps, the flat brown
slap of feet, the worms. She calls it *exile*,
*house arrest, carcass, ruination.*

She murmurs, *In a city of crosses and virgins
trust only the sky, a great blue crusading
for weather.* She calls her life back
each day, its charming fables, its hot walks.

## Tom Collins

The bars were most often nautical: faux portholes, nets tattooed with cork
and fish tanks sunk into the wall, backlit neon tetras, eels—and called
*The Skippers Quarters* or the *Jolly Roger*, skull and cross boned, anchored by
a jukebox playing "Poinciana," "Chances Are" and—in a certain sort of dive—
"I Walk the Line." Adolescent in those lounges, roadhouses of no ID,
her boyfriend and she—not yet eighteen—would sink onto a dark banquette,
nod along with Art Blakey and order a Tom Collins, a Martini.

Years after the Christmas party when they atomized the stereo,
smashing its parts one by one, that was done. Still, in a certain light
in places like this neighborhood saloon where she stopped to have
a quick one after work and grab a six, she can almost see her skinny self,
shoulder blades like sharp wings, thighs stuck to the plastic seat, leaning
into the evening, carefully pulling the little sword of fruit from the Tom Collins,
stripping the orange slice with her teeth, finishing off the cherry.

# The Interview

*What should I ask you instead of these questions? he wanted to
know.*

—William Matthews

*Why do you write?*

On a day of unspeakable sadness—say, this day
when my arms are roped to kitchen machines,
when the space between heartbeats widens
impossibly, another morning in which I make toast,
shuffle to the cat's bowl, start the dishwasher,
on that morning I can still pick up a pen.

*Where do you get your ideas?*

They come in on the red-eye from the coast,
on one crutch, fresh from the hospital,
dazed, dozing, hitching in
on the back of someone else's poem.
They come naturally, artificially, suntanned,
drunk, you can't knock 'em off with a boat paddle.

*What are your influences? What inspires you?*

I'm inspired by the laps I've sat on.
Moved by a caress or two. And by the words
I love. I'm influenced by children, by the spirit,
not religion, by a sidewise view of art.

*And those things you write about....*

When I write summer evenings in the back of a Chevy,
what Bill taught me, the fat professor's poppies,
when I write those jump-up kisses, diving off the buoy,
the pungent tropics, they're all real.

Or almost.

Now you must ask instead, what it means to be born with a caul.
Ask what mountains know about yawns.
Inquire how it felt to walk into the desert further and further
to let a blood-red sunset envelop my shoes like sand.

Ask that.

## The Words for Hot

The roosters call morning from house to house,
light takes the hillside and the only mist
hangs back, coy in the landscape's corners.

All night the cold worried my feet and
I imagined beaches, lay awake
inventing shapes to catch my own blood heat—

too late by then—to trap the afternoon that sizzled
in paving stones, hissed from whitewashed walls.
Instead of that some boneache chill remains.

Tonight, I crave the words for hot not found
in someone else's skin—volcano, sirocco, scorch,
cauldron, August, roast—and know there aren't

enough assorted heats in my one flesh to match
those burning stones, that whitewashed brick.

# Notes

**HOME FIRES**  Achilles's mother Thetis bore six other children, all of whom perished either when she attempted to render them immortal by fire or when she destroyed them.

**FREE FALL**  for Jan

**WOLF**  after Andrea Hollander Budy

**I SWAN**  The epigraph comes from Yeats's poem "Leda and the Swan."

**THE CITY**  The epigraph comes from a writing prompt from Lynn Emanuel.

**TOUCH**  The epigraph comes from Galway Kinnell's poem "Lackawanna."

**WILDCATTING**  for Rhonda

**QUESTIONS**  for Joe Wilfer

**DOG DAYS**  An FM road is a Farm-to-Market road.

**KEEPING UP WITH THE DEAD**  Houdini, a foe of spiritualism, promised his wife that if there were a spirit world as she believed, he would come back after his death to tell her so.

**SAN MIGUEL WIDOW**  for Tamam

# ACKNOWLEDGMENTS

Several of these poems in one form or another appeared in
*Acornwhistle, Athens Avenue: A Collection of Poetry, Borderlands,
Conspire, Isibongo, Maverick, Meridian, Mystic River Review,
Perihelion, PoetryMagazine.com, Prairie Dog, Suite 101,
The Astrophysicist's Tango Partner, Tintern Abbey, 2River View,
Unlikely Stories,* and *Voices International.*

WENDY TAYLOR CARLISLE was born in Manhattan, raised in Bermuda, Connecticut, and Ft. Lauderdale, Florida, and lives now in the Arkansas Ozarks in a house she built in 1980. She has an MA from the University of Arkansas and an MFA from Vermont College of Fine Arts. She is the author of *On the Way to the Promised Land Zoo* (Cyberwit, 2019), *The Mercy of Traffic* (Unlikely Books, 2019), and *Discount Fireworks* (Jacaranda Press, 2008). Chapbooks include *They Went to the Beach to Play* (Locofo Chaps, 2016), *Chap Book* (Platypus Press, 2016), *Persephone on the Metro* (MadHat Press, 2014), *The Storage of Angels* (Slow Water Press, 2008), and *After Happily Ever After* (Two River Chapbooks, 2003). Her collection *The Mercy of Traffic* won the Phillip H. McMath Post-Publication Award.

CPSIA information can be obtained
at www.ICGtesting.com
Printed in the USA
BVHW042249010223
657692BV00004B/82